# How I Became My Own Business

## by Christina E. Rogers

This book is dedicated to three very special people who helped mold the person that I am.

**My mother, Zoë Jackson-Jarra.** You've always allowed me to be myself and you've always showed my sister and I how to be fearless and fabulous while working hard on everything we've ever dreamt of.

**My sister, Ciera Rogers.** Not only are you one of my best friends, you are a daily dose of inspiration that keeps me focused and dedicated.

**In loving memory of my father, Sulayman M. Jarra.** Not a day passes where I don't feel that you are not here and this is the impact I want to leave on the world. Thank you for loving us.

## Introduction

About two and a half years ago, I found myself staring into space while listening to my co-worker complain about her shifts being inconvenient as the time moved slower than molasses. I made about $10 that day at work and I was so frustrated as I walked to my paid meter in the cold that I almost began to cry. Something needed to change. I drove home around 2:25 a.m. daydreaming about the day I would own my own business and finally be free from having to clock into someone else's dream.

At the time, I was in the music business and working at a bar to make ends meet. My music contract crumbled and the $2000 a month I was promised was no longer existent. At that moment I told myself that I would give myself *two* weeks to start a business and be financially on my own without a boss. You may be at a crossroad at this very moment, you may be stressed out, annoyed, frustrated, upset and trying to decide what you're going to do and *how* you're going to do it. I've been at this very point and I can tell you that even though you can't see past the dust, it will clear up and you will prevail.

This booklet is designed to help you by using key points that I learned while reaching my goals as a business owner. I'm not promising that you will be the next millionaire, but if you stick to the key points, I guarantee that something positive will come out of it.

How I Became My Own Business

## Getting Past The "I Think I Can" Attitude

One thing that I had to learn through my "shoot and miss era" was that I couldn't keep doubting myself. Every time I thought something wouldn't work, it didn't. It was that simple. My first business endeavor was a lipstick line called, "**Lipchix**". I used to try to sell lipstick that was already in stores around the United States and call it my own. After running around Downtown, Los Angeles to fill orders, I realized that I only made about $50 after selling 10-15 lipsticks. I came up empty handed every time. I tried to make my packaging cute, I tried to add a special touch by adding personal "thank you" cards and I was spending my profit on all of this stuff without even realizing it.

Once I did realize it, however, I started to feel horrible about my decisions. I started doubting myself and wondering if being a business owner was for me and I eventually started looking for jobs as a leasing agent. I gave up before I even put in the full effort of creating the business. Once I regained my composure, I tried to add jewelry to my lipstick line and failed again. Because my mindset wasn't strong enough, I fell back into the dark hole of not believing in myself. I questioned every decision and I questioned every product I bought.

In order to achieve a goal, you must rid the words "think", "maybe", "can't", "don't", etc... from your vocabulary. You cannot successfully move through cement as a human being. Self doubt is cement to your progression. You have to adopt the ability to say, "I'm able" through tough times. If I had dedicated myself to that business and kept creating new ideas and growing with my mistakes, I would've conquered my goals much earlier than I did.

This week I want to challenge you to try and push past self doubt. Look at the mistakes you've made in your business endeavors, write them down and figure out a solution. Grow with the mistake. It's okay to make mistakes because that helps you move on to something that has the potential to work for you.

## Deciding *What* To Do

I could have beat my head against the wall trying to figure out what would make me some money. I raked my brain daily wondering what was going to finally work for me. This process was difficult and often led to me giving up at the end of the day and trying to find a job. When you're trying to decide what your business should be, be honest with yourself. The worst thing is leaving a job and stepping into another situation that feels like a job. If you don't know what I mean, listen to this...

I moved to Los Angeles in 2012 with the intentions of being my own boss. I then gave up about 11 months later, moved back to Houston, became a leasing agent and then got a contract as a songwriter. Once I got that contract I thought I was good to go. I have a boss, but it's not really a boss because he's my friend. I'm free! I get to work sometimes and get paid for it. *Wrong!* Even though I was doing something that was out of the ordinary, I wasn't happy. I still had to report to someone, I still had to do things I didn't want to do like stay up at all times of the night, mingle with people whom I didn't want to be around, watch people do drugs and drink and damage their bodies and most of all, alter my beliefs and goals to please someone else. Don't sell yourself short when you decide what you will do as a business owner. Be smart about your decision. When choosing a business venture, you have to go with something that is hot on the market. One thing I had to learn was that I was selling to customers and not to myself. Plenty of things that I liked did not work well for my customer base.. One of the top searches in Google at that time was "What do people need?". I had no idea that the answer was in my face, but I had the right idea. I ran myself in circles trying to come up with the solution but at the end of the day I had to learn that if I kept it simple, the sales would come with somewhat of an ease. What are you passionate about? This should most likely begin your entrepreneurial journey.

## Doing Your Own Research

So you're excited and ready to pounce on a few ideas you've been holding onto, but now you have to figure out the smartest way to begin your business. Don't be afraid to research the Internet, read books, get opinions and ask questions but always remember that you are paving your *own* road with your *own* idea. We are all made differently and one man's idea won't necessarily work for another man. When doing research, add your research to your mental catalogue and apply it to your business growth with your own artistic twist and ideas.

In my high school years, a few smart business minded individuals started a line of purses with custom photos on them. I saw the popularity in the items and decided to duplicate them. Needless to say, this was the wrong move. The idea wasn't original, I didn't have a customer base, I created automatic competition within the same circle and I was unsuccessful in the first day of business.

I get a lot of questions about how I started my business and the exact steps I took in order to make it so successful. I primarily shy away from answering these types of questions because I don't want to hand someone my full business, I don't want to give them access to my exact path for them to take it as well and of course I don't want to put a dent in my income.

A mistake that I've made in the past is letting new people in and giving them tips and secrets only to see them create the same exact business, go the same exact places I go to fuel my business, use the same marketing tactics to gain sales and exposure and basically reaching my level without having to do the work to get there.

The best form of knowledge comes from experience. It comes from trial and error and stepping out on thin air to see the outcome. If I have a question about something, I don't ask the nearest human being. I get online and I research the answer from multiple sources and I believe this helped tremendously with the growth of my business.

Nothing makes me more upset than when I'm scrolling on Instagram and see a photo that I shot on someone else's business page promoting the same dress. Nothing makes me want to scream more than going to their website and seeing my pictures that are being used to promote and sell the same item. Not only is it my property, it's my hard work and original idea. When going through your first steps of business, never become desperate enough to leech off of the original idea and production of someone else.

## Focus, Self-Starting & Persistence

A lot of people get excited when they get a day off from work. The number one thing I hear is "I get to sleep in." As a business owner, there is never a chance to "sleep in". I've been programmed to get up early in the morning and begin work. It doesn't matter if I have something to do or not, I get up and create a work day for myself. The most important thing about being a business owner is being a "self-starter". Without this tool, it is less likely that you will be successful.

Most business owners I know, including myself, rarely ever go out every night of the week because they can, rarely ever take a week off because they can and rarely ever slump around because they can. There's nothing more liberating than seeing your seed grow before your eyes so this is motivation in itself. It's not hard to focus on something that you're passionate about.

I'm always excited about new ideas that I have for my business and I can't wait to put them in full effect to see if it helps my business grow or not. This keeps me persistent on the goals that I once had in the beginning. Once I feel myself becoming stagnant and idle, I create a new realm of business for myself. This includes adding something new to my store and thinking of other ways to progress myself or my business.

It helps to create monthly goals for yourself as well. For example, "I'm going to make $3000 this month." Do what is necessary to reach that goal and even if you don't reach it, you've at least made a few changes and tweaks within the business to progress it.

## **Patience**

It is *so* easy to get discouraged when something doesn't work out, especially when you've put everything into it. I'm no stranger to this because I've basically tried it all until I finally reached my goal. I remember sitting back exhausted from spending a full day throwing out ideas, doing research and failing and saying to myself "Just give up."

The beauty in giving up for the day is waking up the next day full of energy to try again. I like to think it's okay to feel discouraged, frustrated or upset about it, but only for a moment. Sometimes you need a break to gain back mental artistry. Fresh ideas come when you're well rested and strapped with positive energy.

We work with more than just ourselves in this world. We're working with a lot of beliefs and ideas about faith, destiny, energy, universe, etc... Just remember to believe that you can achieve your goals and you will. This doesn't come without hard work, though.

Imagine going to the gym once and walking out with the body you went in to achieve. You wouldn't work out anymore and you wouldn't work as hard to achieve a goal you had. Working out is tough and it involves dedication, persistence, focus and a slew of other things. Compare this to business. You're going to get negative feelings from time to time because you're human. As long as you can be patient with yourself and the journey, the outcome will be there. Anything that you want is worth the wait if it means that much to you.

## Behind The Scenes

Once you get the business up and going, you have to make sure that all of your paperwork is in order. Do research to find out the proper documents needed to help your business grow successfully. It's always fun making money and supporting yourself as an owner and CEO but we still owe money to the government at the end of the year and they're still looking for organization within the business. I talk about this a little more in the third section of this book, *"I Started My Business, What Now?"*

You will need a business account that is only used for business purposes, you will need a Tax ID # and also depending on the type of business you own, you will possibly need a sellers permit.

I remember when my business started picking up speed, I was making purchases with my personal account and spending loosely. My sister told me that the money that was being made wasn't mine, it was for the business. This changed my perspective on how I was going about managing my money.

It's always a good idea to have someone who can help you manage the accounting part of the business. If you are capable of doing it yourself, you should definitely keep track of all purchases so that it isn't confusing at the end of the year.

There are multiple streams of marketing that can be used for your business. Social media is a very important stream. I use social media faithfully to promote my brand and market to my customers. One secret that I've learned is to make the marketing feel genuine and not forced. Less is more. For example, when I post a garment from my website on Instagram,, I name the garment and the website and move forward. Chances are, the customer is visual and sees the product they want, goes to the site and buys.

They don't want to read an essay about the product while trying to purchase. They basically want the product handed to them and they want to pay for it and go about their day. Adopt the simple approach and see what it does for your business endeavors.

This also worked for the name of my business. In the beginning it was named *"Cest La Vie Luv"*. Most people don't even know how to pronounce it, let alone how to spell it. I was setting myself up for lots of complications with my customers. It only made sense to change the name of my business to **shopchrisszoe.com** because I was already a brand.

How I Became My Own Business

People knew me as Chriss Zoë. They searched my name already, they followed me on Instagram, Facebook and Twitter and now all they had to do was type "shop" before my name to access my clothing. It was easy and quick and increased my sales tremendously.

## Keeping A Solid Image & Brand

Your image is very important when trying to create and manage a brand. You are your brand; you are the owner. Everything you do has the potential to progress or ruin your brand. You have to place yourself on a high pedestal. Begin making business savvy decisions in your everyday lifestyle and think like a boss.

"If I post this on my social media outlet, is it going to hurt my business?"

I keep most of my private life away from social media because I understand how important my image is and how it can affect my income. Your customers make up the entire world and this includes tons of different beliefs, morals, values, goals, walks of life, etc... Become your brand and make it a priority from day to day.

We've all seen it happen before. A celebrity has an endorsement and does something that gets him or her in trouble with the law or their spouses. Endorsers begin to snatch away contracts because their brands are too important to displease the customers. Displeased customers end in plunging sales and less loyalty.

Your brand should feel safe and consistent to a customer. They should always know that if they need a certain something they can come to you to get it. For me, this is a basic, comfortable dress. I've pushed my brand out under that umbrella and stuck to the same thing for three years and this has been successful for me.

Once you get the hang of something and it becomes your stamp, branch out from there. When I first began my store I sold stretchy tank dresses in every color under the sun. From there I branched off to leggings and two pieces and then to casual dresses. My bread and butter was the stretchy tank dress, though. Find your bread and butter and continue to build from there, but always remember your image and branding!

# How I Doubled My Sales

**Section 2**

## Introduction

In June 2014, I started my business from $200 and an Instagram following and that was *way* better than waiting tables at a bar on Hollywood Blvd in my opinion. I used to come home with $10-$50 in tips and that wasn't even enough to help me pay for my Starbucks habit. I have to admit that I knew nothing about business or even how to run a business properly so I was literally running my business off of how the wind blew on that particular day. All I really cared about was the income that the business was bringing me and that I didn't have to clock in to my bar gig ever again. Oh, and that I could now indulge in my daily runs to the very rambunctious Starbucks freely.

In the last section, *How I Became My Own Business*, I explained my experiences with starting my business and all of the mental barriers I had to jump over to achieve success in it. What I didn't let you in on is how I took $2000 in sales a month to $4000 in sales the very next month and eventually $20,000 in sales minimum a month. What a difference! In this section, I'm going to let you in on several secrets that will most likely help you take your business to the next level. Take a seat, grab a cup of your favorite beverage and let this soak in, because it's gonna be good.

## Bread & Butter

Your business needs to be known for something. This "something" is a product that your customers come to you for specifically because that's what they know you for. For me, it's comfortable and stretchy outfits. My customers know that if they want to find a basic product that they can rely on, they can come to me. If you get rid of this item, you might as well start all over. For example, if you are a makeup artist and you build your customer base and then switch to being a hairstylist and expect your business to remain the same, you will be very disappointed.

Once you have your bread and butter, find ways to make it interesting. Your bread and butter gets the customers hooked in and leads them to other products or services that you offer. Once your customer is hooked in, you can understand what they are there for. Venture out by creating a different version of your bread and butter.

For example, I started with short tank dresses and eventually I realized that my customer base had grown and they already had my "bread and butter product" so I decided to make long tank dresses to capitalize. This, for me, was very successful.

Always remember that you have to try something first in order to fail. Never doubt an idea that you have before you actually put in the time and effort to do it.

## Social Media Influence

Social Media definitely plays a big part in your branding. If your following is great on social media, you have a fan base. This fan base is a potential customer base. I got my fan base by doing impersonations of Beyonce and also by doing music. From there, I created my line and had loyal customers who have supported me ever since. For some, it isn't like this.

Once you understand the concept of creating a fan base and going from there, this will be much easier to achieve. There are tons and tons of people who are starting to use their social media status to get recognition and start businesses. They tap into that little talent they had when they were in High School and transform it into something that not even an entry level corporate worker can achieve. It's definitely possible.

The most important part of creating your social media influence is by having something to influence with. There are some people who use their looks, there are some people who use their voice and there are some people who use their kids. There's a hustle everywhere you look.

Ask yourself what makes your different from the next person and use that to your ability. If you can knit a mean scarf, use it. What's so special about you? Once you figure it out, apply it to your fan base. If it doesn't stick, they don't like it. Don't get emotional and run to the ice cream; just pick a new trait, start over and try to stick it again.

Social media has seen it all, so be creative. Always remember that the quickest way to fail is to follow in someone else's footsteps.

## Promotional Humans

If nobody is sporting your product, how is it going to be noticed? As the famous cliché goes: "To make money, you have to spend money."

At this moment our lives are powered and driven by images. Ever since apps like Instagram and Snapchat came around, we've been contorting our bodies and faces to make an impression on the world so we can see that people like it and have something to say. This makes us very vain.

Use this to your advantage. If you understand that people just want to look good, use someone who wants to look good and put your product in their hand. The only catch is that they have to promote your services for your generosity. Nothing is free in this world, though, so a few may try to hit you with a bill. You make the decision if it's worth it.

I remember when I had just moved to Los Angeles and I went out to eat with my sister and her best friend. When we walked in there were a group of girls taking pictures in the middle of the walkway. They were sucking their full bellies in, poking their hips out, pointing their toes and basically doing whatever it took to get a good image. I remember thinking that they looked like clowns and I told myself that I would never be that way.

Two years later, I was that girl in the middle of the restaurant trying to get a good picture because if I didn't, I wouldn't make my sales increase. A big part of making sales, is staying consistent. I used to post photos every single day and night so my followers would remember me and my product.

If you post every two weeks, you're only going to get attention every two weeks. It's sad, but it's true. I decided to separate my business page and my personal page so that I could create space between the two. On my personal page, I post 1-3 times a day to get my business page recognition, but on my business page I post up to 15 times a day to keep my income flowing. This has definitely increased my sales.

## Promotional Sales

Sales can be good and sales can be bad. When I say "sales", I mean "discounts". Sometimes when I'm having a bad week, I create a sale. Below are a few pros and cons of doing this.

**Pros:**

-Increase in business

-I'm able to get rid of inventory

-I have new customers

**Cons:**

- Same amount of profit as a normal day

- When I do too many sales, my customers hold out until the next one because they know it's coming soon I create more work for myself. I know of a store I used to frequent in Los Angeles that added the "sale trick" into their daily business tactics. Sales make people buy quicker because they think they're getting a deal, right? Well, this particular store used to greet you when you walked in and then hit you with, "Everything is 20% off!". Now, you're more inclined to buy because the pretty dress on the mannequin isn't $45.99, it's really $36.79. Smart, right?

## Contests

If you're having trouble getting traffic to your profile, you may want to incorporate a little thing called contests. At one point I offered my customers a free item of their choice. The only catch was that they had to tag me and tell me what they wanted by posting it to their Instagram profiles. The customers who participated were probably intrigued because they wanted to win a dress they have been eyeing so they posted it without hesitation. Bingo!

This gave me access to their followers, friends *and* haters. In return, I got traffic and I got plenty of sales for the day and for a few days after. There are never too many contests because people love free stuff! People might even like to be a little competitive, too!

Recently I created another contest that involved limited access. I told my customers that only a certain amount of them could access this golden ticket to get a crazy discount at my store. This caused quick sales because they rushed to try and grab their spot before there weren't anymore tickets left. Creativity is key when you do anything with your business. The more fun you have with it, it will show and your customers will want to have fun with you!

## Quick Services

When I get an order and ship it quickly, my sales with that particular customer have the potential of remaining and becoming consistent. Customers love when they request something and it's done quickly. Think about it. When you order something from an online store, wouldn't you rather a 2-day wait time opposed to a 2 week wait time? Yeah, me too!

Sometimes life happens and gets in the way of your rapidity, but at least make an effort during normal times to get your product out to your customer quickly. Trust me, they will appreciate it and spread the word to their friends and family.

When they spread the word, this brings your more traffic, more business, more sales and more trips to Starbucks!

This applies to business emails, too! Customers appreciate quick responses and even quicker problem solving. I've been in customer service for a very long time, even outside of my business. I used to be a server so I used to move so fast in order to keep my peace with my customers because I relied on my tip at the end of their meal. This is sort of the same concept. Your customer requests your service, you dash off to handle your business, you bring your customer the product that they ordered without mistake (but we're only human so these occur sometimes) and you receive your reward for doing so. For you and I, this is a happy customer and a promising return for our businesses.

## Email Marketing

Almost everyone has an email account in 2016. If they don't, it's as strange as a bird with a skirt on. When you utilize this feature for sales growth, you can really benefit from the results. Use websites like mailchimp.com to create email blasts for your products. Chances are that not everyone will see your posts on Instagram or Facebook or Twitter, so meet them somewhere else.

People check their email for business purposes and for other reasons as well. Why not be one of those reasons? Email blasts remind your customers that you are there and ready to accept them into your business.

Always remember to be creative when making email blasts. Make them clean and to the point, but use a catchy subject title to get the customer interested. Sometimes when I'm scrolling through my email account, I see a catchy phrase like, "Here's $1000!". I stop scrolling and then I realize that it's a scam. Most scam artists use money to get you hooked on to their scheme and sometimes it actually works.

Why not use the same types of methods to get your customers' attention? "Hey! Here's $20 towards [your business name here]!" It's okay to bribe them a little bit, but never lead them to false information because that breaks the trust factor. Your customers must trust you and also feel comfortable with your product and service.

## Outro

When you apply all this and more to your business strategy, you will indeed see some major changes in your business. These strategies worked really well for me on my way up from the bottom and I hope that it does the same for you. Being in business is not so easy when you don't know where to start so I hope my words of experience teach you something that you've never quite realized.

Before I go, I want to add one more strategy to all the other ones. Try envisioning yourself in your goals every chance you get. If you want a fur coat, envision yourself putting on a fur coat every single time you place a jacket over your shoulders. If you want a million dollars in the bank, imagine your bank statement with seven figures on it when you look at it.

All of our dreams and goals start with ourselves and our ability to actually do it. Being positive and imagining these things before they happen play a huge part in them actually happening. Create a vision board with your goals on them in picture form or word form and look at it every morning before you start your day. Organize your business goals so that they're easier to see, understand and execute. Most of all, have fun and be creative when you're doing something you love. This will definitely rub off on your customers! Happy Entrepreneurship!

If you'd like to shop my website, visit shopchrisszoe.com or follow us on Instagram at @shopchrisszoe.

# I Started My Business!

## *What Now?*

**Section 3**

## First Thing Is First...

Now that you have your business name and idea, it's time to complete a few things.

**Come up with a logo for your brand**. Branding is very important for your business. When someone sees your logo, they have to instantly be able to connect it with your business. Your logo will go on your website, emails, packaging and other important things for your business. If you're crafty with the computer and have an idea what you want your logo to be, take a stab at making it by using websites like *PicMonkey.com*. If you aren't crafty and need help, you can use websites like *elance.com*. On ELance, you can hire a professional to do the logo for you.

**Buy a domain name.** Unfortunately, the biggest turn-off is when I visit a website that shows who it's hosted by. It makes me leery of purchasing because maybe the store isn't all the way together yet, maybe it's a scam and a slew of other worries. Having a domain name makes you official and it has a more professional appearance. A domain shouldn't cost you more than $20 a year. Whomever you use to host your website will have a list of domain name providers to choose from and they'll even help you set it up. If you aren't tech savvy, no worries, they have geeks who will do it for you.

**Create a business email.** Your domain provider will most likely have an option for you to create a business email. The more professional emails are the emails containing the website.com. *Ex:* info@yourwebsite.com

**Find a eCommerce hosting website.** I started off using **BigCartel.com** as a website host. Five free products are allowed before they begin charging monthly, tons of website themes are available for purchase and for free and it's super easy to get started using. Over time I realized that **Shopify.com** may be the best option for me. They have more business tools to offer that will help you in the long run including more professional website themes, apps that do the work for you, apps that help build your business, newsletters that help you grow your business and so many other features that really show you that they care about the growth of your business. I pay about $40 a month to use Shopify and it's totally worth it. Some apps cost money, but they are good for business (I'll list some great apps in the next chapter).

**Create social media outlets.** The most crucial tool this day in time is social media. Everyone from kids to grannies have a social media account whether it's **Facebook.com** , **Instagram.com** or **Twitter.com** . I suggest that you immediately start your business accounts when you begin your business so that they can grow together. Posting on those social media outlets will help your business tremendously. Instagram has made it possible to easily switch back and forth between accounts which help out while promoting your business daily.

**Business Cards.** It's always good to have business cards just incase you have a potential customer during your daily operations. You can get business cards made pretty much anywhere these days but **VistaPrint.com** is where I choose to shop at. There are always promotional discounts and there's a ton of options to choose from. If you aren't tech savvy and can't even begin to create your own business card layout, VistaPrint has professionals that are able to help you.

Once you're done with these steps, it's time to move on to the next important steps!

## Apps To Success ( *Shopify Only*)

If you don't plan on using Shopify.com as a eCommerce hosting site, go ahead and skip to the next chapter. If you are currently using or plan on using Shopify.com I'll name some handy apps that I use as my business tools. You can find these in the app store on Shopify.

**Fomo.** This app is used to let your visitors and potential customers know that something was purchased by a customer in a certain location. In doing this, it promotes recently bought items during the whole visit and it potentially increases sales due to "fear of missing out". This app is around **$14 a month** .

**Has It Shipped Yet.** I use this app to let my customers find their own tracking information on my website. This decreases the amount of questions in my email inbox asking where their orders are. Customers (and us alike) get excited once they purchase something and they can't wait to get it. Instead of going through the hassle of looking up the customer's order and searching for tracking information and then emailing them back with this information, this app makes it easy to focus on other things. This app is *free* on the shopify app store.

**KIT.** " Keep In Touch" is the most needed app for me because when your store is doing well, it does all the work for you. KIT will text message you in the morning and go over stats with you, suggest ads for email blasts, facebook posts or instagram and will even let you know how your sales were for the month and help you budget for future ads. If KIT doesn't reach out and you want something all you have to say is, "Hi Kit!" and the rest is just simply up to you. KIT is **$20 a month** and totally worth it.

**MailChimp.** Connecting MailChimp to your Shopify website will help you out tremendously when you're ready to send out email blasts. When a customer visits your store and enters their email address to subscribe to news, MailChimp will automatically add it to your list. You can manually create email blasts, schedule them for a later date or just keep your email subscribers in a safe place for the future. You can also manually add subscribers. This service is *free*.

**Out Of Stock by OG.** This app helps keep your store clean and organized. When an item is out of stock, this app simply hides it from your potential customers. The service is completely *free*.

**Popups, Promos & Banners- Pixelpop.** This pop up comes alive when your potential customer visits your website. You can tell about a new product, offer a discount or ask them to sign up for your email list. This service is **free-$48** a month. Pricing depends on how many people will see your pop up a month. **Shippo.** If you plan on shipping out product, shippo makes it easy for you to do so. All you have to do is connect your store to this service and it automatically imports your orders. Once that happens you're able to ship bulk orders, international (or you may use Stamps.com which has cheaper rates for international customers) or do them separately. This service is *free*.

How I Became My Own Business

## Mastering Products & Product Shots

**Product & Website Professionalism.**

When I first began my business, I simply took a Sony camera, took my product out of it's packaging, put it on and shot it. From there, I put it on my website and it sold. Later on down the line, I craved more professionalism. It was almost embarrassing when people went to my website and saw me as the model on top of my apartment building roof doing the best I could.

I had to learn that the more professionalism I had, the more I would lean towards a quality customer base. This is important to you because you want customers who are equally happy about your work. They always say that quality is better than quantity and it proved right once I began seeing plenty of sales and plenty of problems that came with it. I preferred customers that would enjoy my product and pay for it. **Product Perfection.** This brings me to another point. Your product has to be something that you are proud of and in return your customers will be gracious and continue to support you. Take the time to build your product and make it your precious little baby until it's time to release it into the wild. You'll be happier and more comfortable with the fact that you released something you love than the fact that you released something that you would have requested a refund for yourself!

**Clothing Labels.** If you are selling clothing and you are looking for labels, **DutchLabels.com** is a good place to look. All you have to do is upload a design, pick a label style and decide if you want the label to iron on or if you want to sew it on.

**Product Shots.** If you cannot work a camera well enough, hire a photographer for product shots. Product shots require the right amount of light, the right angles and the right camera to be honest. I've been frustrated with product shots for years until I finally hired a photographer. With a white background, it was easy to see the product and the professional camera made the product look amazing.

**Product Shots RELOADED.** Unfortunately my customers didn't appreciate my clothing without a body in it. It made it hard for them to imagine themselves in the clothing. From there, I

How I Became My Own Business

hired models and put their bodies in the clothing. From there, I realized that even though the body was in the clothing, my customers needed to visualize themselves in a scenery. From there I put my models outside in the real world.

## **Shipping & Packaging**

It took me a while to complete my packaging and honestly I'm still working on it because I'm never satisfied. At first, I used to take my product and put it in a USPS flat rate envelope and ship it off. After a while, I wasn't satisfied with the way it looked. It was a challenge figuring out USPS' package policies, figuring out how to print labels and figuring out the best method of shipping. I've placed tips below to make it a little easier for you.

**Shipping.**

*USPS Shipping (this is what I use)*

If you are using a **flat rate envelope**, make sure that the contents first fit in the envelope before making the label. If you'd prefer to use a **polybag** ( *and the same applies to boxes*) instead of the flat rate envelope, always make sure that when you create labels, you give the *dimensions of the package* and *weight of the product*. Upon entering this information, USPS will charge you the correct amount and all you will have to do is drop it at the postal service.

**Label Making.** I order paper for my labels online at ebay.com. I simply search for "self adhesive shipping labels" and I choose labels with 2 labels per sheet. I found 1000 labels online for roughly $35.

**Laser Printer.** The best printer for the job is a laser printer. It's quicker and the ink doesn't run out as quickly as regular printing ink. The ink, however, is about $200 but I'm sure it can be found cheaper online. I use the Canon Laser Printer. **Product Tags.** If you sell clothing and want tags to accompany your product, an easier method could be making business card style cards online, buying a hole puncher and a tagging gun. *Wallah!* There's a product tag hack for you!

**Packaging Letters & Promotional Items.** My best friend has literally been PicMonkey.com and VistaPrint.com when it comes to making promotional items for my store. Some good ideas are as follows:

- *Discount cards* - Including discount cards in your package help your customers return to your store and purchase more from you.

- *Thank you cards*- Always thank your customers for purchasing from you because it's just the polite thing to do. Aside from that, customers appreciate being thanked. They've supported your business and they want to feel like they received great service.

- *Promotional gifts* - Can you imagine opening up an order and receiving something extra that you didn't ask for? That feeling alone would make you feel great about your purchase. VistaPrint has tons of promotional items from pens to tablets that you can customize for your business.

- *Stickers* - A sticker would be perfect to "seal" your package or seal your wrapping paper inside the package. This adds more branding to your package so that the customer knows automatically who the package is coming from *and* all the hands that touch the package and all the eyes that see the package will see your sticker on the outside as well which leads to more potential customers.

## The Tough Stuff

Okay, so I had to get slapped against the head with all this information to really understand it. Business owners tried to help me out and explain this to me, but I really didn't understand it until it finally applied to me. This is *really* important for government purposes, so I suggest it be taken serious.

### Step One
### Register your business name!

In order for your business to be taken seriously in "grown up government world" it's a good idea to register the name and get a **DBA** (" *Doing Business As*"). In Houston, TX a DBA can be purchased for $16 at the courthouse. Step Two
Open a business account!

It's a great idea to start a business account in order to separate your personal expenses from your business expenses. This is easier to file during tax season. You have an eye on all business expenses instead of stressing out and trying to separate it all at the end of the year. You will receive a business EIN Tax number which you will need for important tax documents and other verification processes.

### Step Three
### Monthly Business Logging

It's very easy to get caught up in your business tasks and goals and it's possible to get unorganized quickly. If you aren't aware of your expenses and your profit, you will never realize if your business is making money or not. You will also lose track of what's harming your business and what's helping your business. Luckily, there's tools on Shopify.com that help you with this. On your dashboard, it breaks down business profits, where people are buying from, most popular items, etc... This helps with end of the year filing as well. Other eCommerce websites may or may not have these tools, but I'm only using Shopify as an example since I use them.

Other programs can be used like Excel (if you prefer to log manually), physical logging books or other accounting programs available in the form of apps or computer programs.

## Step Four
## You Need A Savings Account!

When you open your business account, you may get a free savings account with it. *Use it!* This comes in handy when taxes are due. Always put aside money in order to pay your taxes at the end of the year, for promotional reasons or simply just to put back into the business. If you aren't good with saving money, incorporate apps like ***Digit*** which helps by taking a small amount of money out of your account each day and saving it for you.

Tip: Always remember that the money that your business makes isn't your own money. It may be best if you put aside the money and pay yourself monthly.

## **Helpful Tips**

***Stay creative***: The most annoying thing about creating is that sooner or later someone is going to copy the things that made you who you are. Every original idea has knock offs. This is why it's always important to stay creative. Do what you have to do to keep creating new and fresh ideas and products for your customer base. They're worth it.

***Stay busy:*** Always remember that if you aren't busy, your business won't be either. There's always something to do! If you feel like there isn't anything to do, create a few tasks to help your business grow, organize your books, create a new website, learn how to do something that contributes to your business, etc... ***Stay relevant:*** Your business requires branding and most importantly you are your brand. That's why it's always great to have some sort of presence and it's even better to have some chatter about you. Every time something dies down in "Kardashian" world, you see a situation occur which brings another wave of chatter which puts the attention on them and in return promotes their brand. I understand that we aren't Kardashians and never will be ( *Never say never because Blac Chyna did it!*) but apply this method to your own brand in a different manner.

***Stay positive***: Business isn't always going to be great. You're going to run into some tough spots that make you question if you even want to have your own business anymore, but everything happens for a damn good reason. Take the trial and make triumph out of it. I'll let you in on a personal business fluke I had recently. During Black Friday 2016 I expected my sales to *finally* pick back up after a long dry spell. Well, they picked up but I had a bad run in with almost every single wholesaler I had. Because of this, tons of orders were late, tons of customers were upset, tons of refunds were given out and on top of plenty of other things, tons of tears fell from my eyes. I wanted to give up and shut my business down forever but instead, I took a step back and invested in my business in order to make it better and prepare for next Black Friday! Positivity works.

***Stay disciplined***: If you don't work, your business doesn't work. Make sure to set goals for yourself and your business daily. Come up with new ways to promote your business so that your customers are always interested.

***Stay aware***: Do you know what your customers want? Do you know where your customers live? Do you know the temperature outside their window? All this is detrimental to your business. It's easy to find this information with social media outlets and eCommerce hosting. Instagram lets you get a detailed glimpse of your stats and so does Shopify. Take the time and do research on your customers and what they want. You can even do a survey via Instagram or Facebook asking what they want you to sell more of. It works!

How I Became My Own Business

Good Luck!

I hope you enjoyed this book and I hope it gets you off to a great start with your business. Always remember that you are the owner of your own business now so you get to call the shots. The amount of work you put into your business will show as you offer your product to your customers so make sure that you take your time and that you're happy with it. *Never chase money, chase your dreams!*

XO,

How I Became My Own Business

How I Became My Own Business